PEGASUS ENCYCLOPEDIA LIBRARY

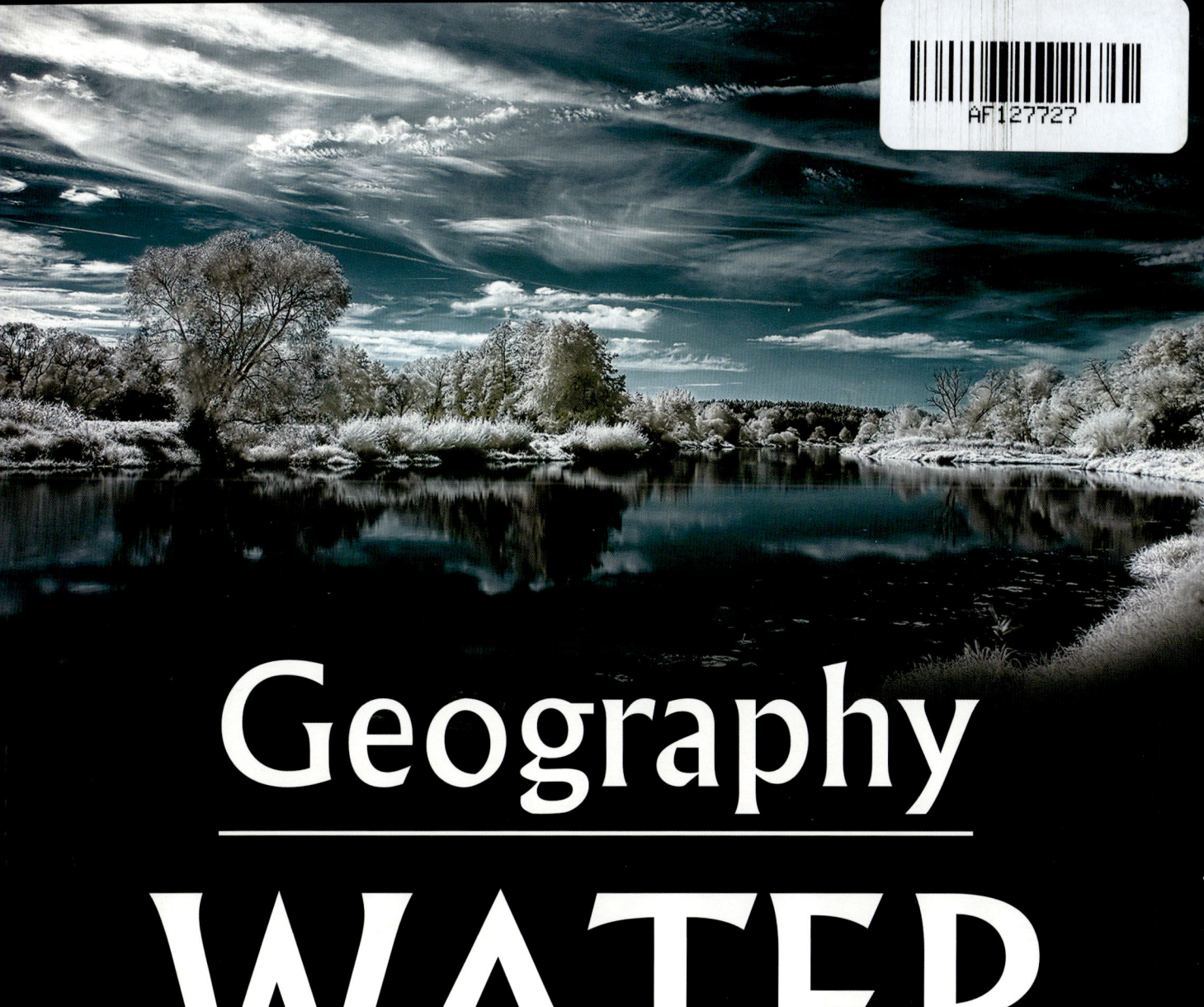

Geography
WATER

Edited by: Pallabi B. Tomar, Hitesh Iplani
Managing editor: Tapasi De
Designed by: Vijesh Chahal, Anil Kumar, Rohit Kumar
Illustrated by: Suman S. Roy, Tanoy Choudhury
Colouring done by: Vinay Kumar, Kiran Kumari & Pradeep Kumar

WATER

CONTENTS

What is a water body? 3

Types of water bodies 4

Test Your Memory 31

Index 32

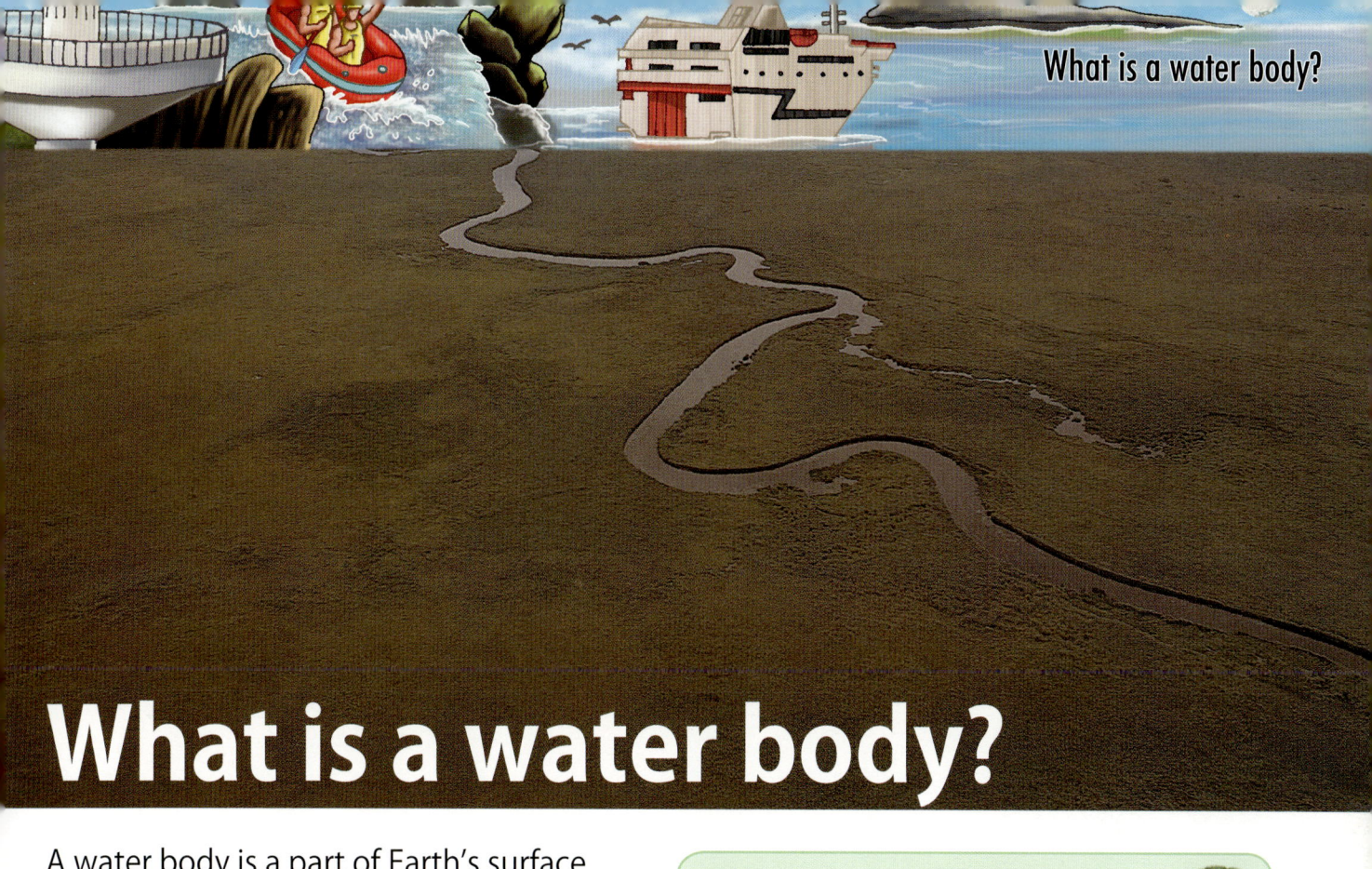

What is a water body?

A water body is a part of Earth's surface covered by a significant amount of water. Generally, the term body of water is used for large gatherings of water, such as oceans, seas and lakes; however, it can also refer to small pools of water such as ponds, puddles, swamps, marshes etc. These water bodies hold water at one place, whereas water bodies like rivers, streams, etc. collect and move water from one place to another. A river moves towards the sea or the ocean after originating from its source.

Bodies of water which are navigable, that is, which allow boats or ships and other sort of vessels to sail through them, are called waterways.

Some bodies of water are artificial, that is, they are made by human-beings for various uses. Examples of man-made water bodies include reservoirs, harbours, canals, etc.

Types of water bodies

Based on the above discussions, we can safely classify water bodies into two different categories— water bodies which only hold water, i.e. **stationary water bodies** and water bodies which hold and move water from one place to another, i.e. **flowing water bodies**.

Stationary water bodies

Stationary water bodies can be further divided into following categories:

1. **Large salt water bodies**
2. **Smaller salt water bodies**
3. **Lakes and ponds**
4. **Wetland**

    Large salt water bodies include ocean, sea and gulf. Smaller salt water bodies include bay, cove, channel, fjord, lagoon, sound, and strait. Lakes and ponds include mere, billabong, crater lake, plunge pool, pond, tarn etc. Wetlands include swamp, bog and marsh.

> The oceans of our planet Earth are unique in our Solar System. No other planet in our Solar System has liquid water.

Large salt water bodies

Ocean

Ocean is a huge body of salt water. Oceans cover approximately 70.9% of the Earth's surface. Ocean is a continuous body of water that has been divided into several other oceans and smaller seas.

    Average depth of an ocean is 3000 m. Average oceanic salinity is around 3.5%. The main body of ocean has been divided into following smaller oceanic regions: Pacific Ocean, Atlantic Ocean, Indian Ocean, Antarctic Ocean (Southern Ocean), which covers the waters that surround Antarctica

Types of water bodies

Astonishing fact

Did you know that the first forms of life on Earth originated in the seas?

Tide pools are rocky pools formed near the sea shore that are filled with seawater. These pools are visible only at low tide.

The Pacific and Atlantic may be further subdivided by the equator into northern and southern portions. Smaller regions of the oceans are called seas, gulfs, bays, straits etc.

The oceans contain roughly 97% of the Earth's water supply.

Sea

A **sea** is a large body of salt water connected with an ocean. It is also used sometimes to describe a large saline lake that lacks a natural outlet, such as the Caspian Sea.

5

WATER

Gulf

A **gulf** is larger than bay and is mostly surrounded by land with a narrow entrance. It is almost like a big lake attached to a large body of water.

The Gulf of Mexico is the largest gulf in the world. The Gulf of Mexico covers approximately 1.6 million sq km. Its deepest part measures 4,383 m at the Sigsbee Deep.

> A cove is a circular or oval inlet on the coast with a narrow entrance; some coves are also referred to as bays.

Cove

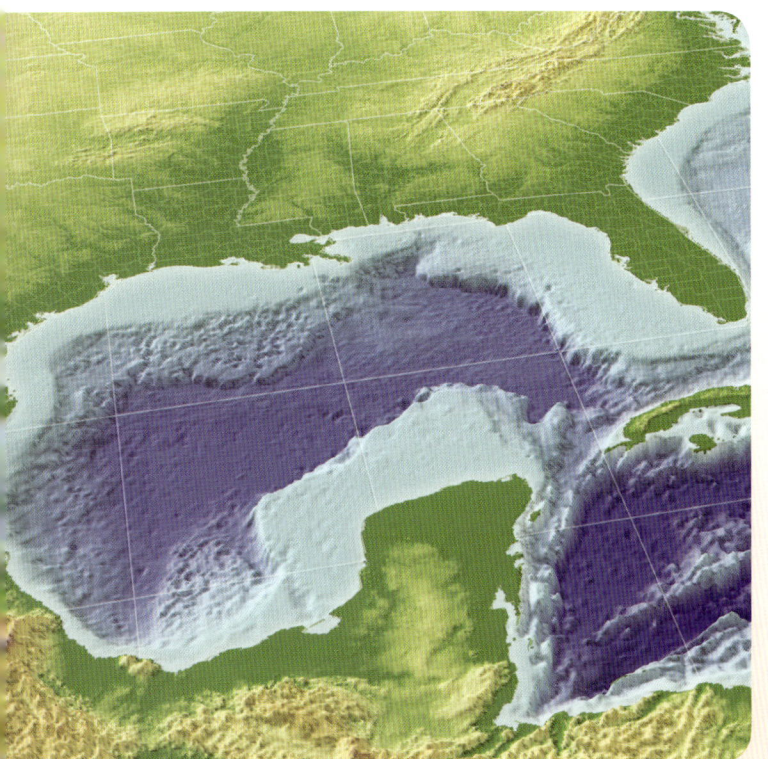

Gulf of Mexico (satellite view)

Smaller salt water bodies

Bay

Bay is a wide semicircular area of water that is partially surrounded by land. They are larger than a cove but smaller than a gulf. A bay has a much wider mouth than a gulf.

The land around bays and gulfs reduces energy of the winds and the sea waves that strike the shore. As a result bays and gulfs generally have calmer waters than the surrounding sea.

Bays are usually formed due to the erosion caused by waves of the softer rocks

Types of water bodies

on a coast. Also, a rise in the water level of a sea can result in the flooding of the shore and creation of a bay.

The Bay of Bengal located in the north-eastern part of the Indian Ocean is the world's largest bay with an area of 2.2 million sq km. It has a depth up to 5,258 m. It is bordered by Bangladesh, India, Sri Lanka and the Andaman and Nicobar Islands.

The Hudson Bay in Canada is the longest bay. Its shoreline is 12,268 km long.

WATER

Sound

Sound is a sea or ocean inlet larger than a bay, deeper and wider than a fjord. A sound is often formed by the sea flooding a river valley. This produces a long inlet where the sloping valley hillsides descend to the sea-level and continue beneath the water to form a sloping sea floor.

Sound fjord

Inlet

An **inlet** is a narrow water body which moves towards the land from a larger water body. It usually leads to an enclosed body of water such as a sound, bay, lagoon or a marsh.

On sea coasts an inlet usually refers to the actual connection between a bay and the ocean and is often called an **entrance**.

Strait

A **strait** is a narrow, navigable channel of water that connects two larger navigable bodies of water. It most commonly refers to a channel of water that lies between two land masses, but it may also refer to a navigable channel through a body of water that is otherwise not navigable, for example because it is too shallow or because it contains reef or an archipelago.

Satellite view of a strait

Man-made channels called canals have also been constructed to connect two bodies of water over land. Although, rivers and canals often provide passage between two large lakes or a lake and a sea, they are not straits. The term strait is used for

Inlet

8

Types of water bodies

much larger, wider features of the marine environment.

Channel

A **channel** is the deeper part of an ocean, sea or strait. It can be both natural and man-made. Its depth is relatively more than the body of water around it.

A channel connects two bodies of water allowing vessels to navigate. Since it provides a shortcut route it helps in saving time and fuel. The term channel can also refer to the course of a river or an ocean strait.

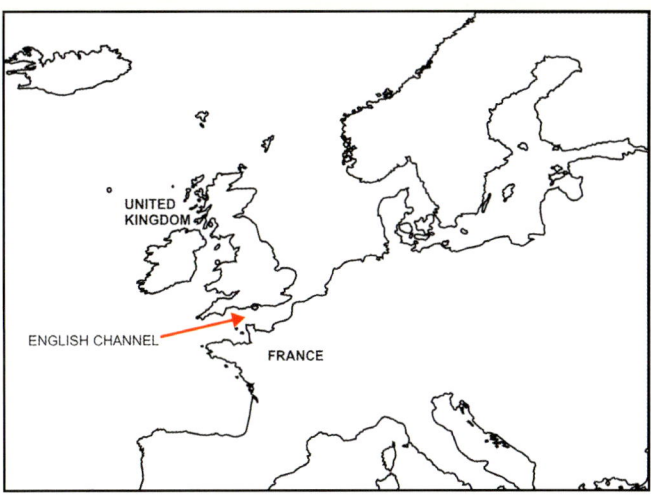

English Channel

WATER

Fjord

Sometimes a sound is formed by a glacier carving out a valley and then receding or the sea invading a glacier valley. The glacier produces a sound (body of water) that often has steep, near vertical, sides that extend deep under water. This type of sound is called a **fjord** (or fiord).

Fjord

Lagoon

A body of relatively shallow salt water separated from the deeper sea by a sand bar, a barrier island or enclosed by a coral reef, or any other such feature is called a **lagoon**.

The world's largest lagoon Grand Lagoon Sud is located in the French territory of New Caledonia.

New Caledonia Lagoon

10

Types of water bodies

Lake

Lakes and ponds

Lake

A **lake** is a body of fresh or salt water of a significant size surrounded by land. Lakes occur inland and are not part of the ocean bodies. Lakes are larger and deeper than ponds. Most lakes are fed and drained by rivers and streams.

Natural lakes are generally found in mountainous areas and areas with ongoing glaciations. Many lakes are artificially constructed for industrial, agricultural use, for hydro-electric power generation or for domestic water supply. Lakes are constructed for the purpose of beautification and enjoyment as well.

Salt lakes form where there is no natural outlet for the water or where the water evaporates rapidly. Small, crescent-shaped lakes called oxbow lakes can form in river valleys. A slow-moving river forms a twisted shape as the outer side of bends are eroded away more rapidly than the

> A mere is a lake that is broader in width than it is deep.

11

WATER

inner side. Finally, a bend in the shape of a horseshoe is formed and the river cuts through the narrow neck. This new passage then forms the main passage for the river thus forming a bow-shaped lake.

> Finland is known as 'the land of thousand lakes'. There are 187,888 lakes in Finland!

Billabong

Billabongs are small lakes which are formed when the path of a stream or a river changes, leaving the former branch with a dead end. Billabongs fill with water seasonally and remain dry for a greater part of the year.

Crater lakes

Crater lakes are formed in volcanic craters and calderas which fill up with water from rainfall more rapidly than they empty through evaporation. For example, the

Lake Superior

Types of water bodies

Crater Lake, Oregon

Crater Lake in Oregon, located within the caldera of Mount Mazama.

> **Lake Vostok in Antarctica is the largest subglacial lake in the world.**

Mill pond

A **mill pond** is any body of water used as a reservoir for a water-powered mill. Mill ponds were often created through the construction of a mill dam across a waterway. In many places, the name Mill Pond name has got stuck with the place though the mill has long since gone.

13

WATER

Moat

Moat

A **moat** is a deep, wide ditch, usually filled with water that surrounds a building or a place. In earlier times it was used to provide initial protection for castles. Later on, their construction and use became primarily for the purpose of beautification.

Plunge pool

A **plunge pool** is a stream pool, lake or pond that is smaller in diameter, but is very deep. Plunge pools are usually formed under the force of a natural factor, such as a waterfall or rapids, but they can also form as a result of man-made objects such as spillways and bridge abutments. The swirling water, sometimes carrying rocks within it, erodes the riverbed into a basin. Plunge pools often remain even after a waterfall has stopped or a stream has changed its course.

Reflecting pool

A **reflecting pool** is a pool often used in

Reflecting pool

Plunge pool

memorials or any other building purely for ornamental purposes. It generally consists of a shallow pool of water usually quite calm. It is built in such away that the structure alongside which it is constructed gets reflected in the water of the pool.

Swimming pool

A **swimming pool** is a container filled with water intended for swimming or water-based enjoyment. A pool can be built either above or in the ground and from materials such as metal, plastic, fibreglass or concrete.

Public pools are used by the general public and private pools are used

Swimming pool

WATER

exclusively by a few people or are built in homes. Many health clubs, fitness centres and private clubs have public pools used mostly for exercise.

Many hotels and Spa resorts have public pools for relaxation. Hot tubs and spas are pools with hot water used for relaxation or therapy and are common in homes, hotels, clubs and resorts. Swimming pools are also used for diving and other water sports, as well as for the training of lifeguards and astronauts.

Pond

A **pond** is a body of standing water, either natural or man-made that is usually smaller than a lake. A wide variety of man-made bodies of water are classified as ponds, including water gardens, water features etc. Ponds are almost always designed for the purpose of beautification.

Fish ponds are used for fish breeding.

A fish pond

Puddle

A **puddle** is a small gathering of water on a surface. They are often formed anywhere

Astonishing fact
In the Oxfordshire town of Wallingford there has been a puddle on the pavement at an intersection since April 1976!

A pond

A cirque is a semi-circular depression in a mountain with steep walls formed as a result of eroding activity of a glacier.

from rain water, in gardens from irrigation and on municipal streets from runoff.

A puddle is small enough for an adult to step over and shallow enough to walk through.

Tarn

A **tarn** is a mountain lake or pool formed in a cirque by a glacier. A moraine may form a natural dam below a tarn.

Vernal pools

Vernal pools (or ephemeral pools), are temporary pools of water without any fish and thus allow the safe development of amphibians and insect species. Most pools are dry for at least part of the year and fill with the winter

Cirque

A moraine is an accumulation of stones and debris formed due to the moving of a glacier mass.

Tarn

WATER

Some pools may remain at least partially filled with water over the course of a year or more, but all vernal pools dry up periodically.

They are called vernal pools because they are often, but not necessarily, at their peak depth in the spring. Despite being dry at times, once filled, they teem with life. The most obvious inhabitants are various species of frogs and toads. Some salamanders also utilize vernal pools for reproduction, but the adults may visit the pool only briefly. In some vernal pools, tadpole shrimp are also common.

Reservoir

A reservoir is a sort of an artificial lake used to store water. Reservoirs are constructed in river valleys by the construction of a dam or by digging in the ground.

Valley dammed reservoir: A dam constructed in a valley relies on the natural surroundings to provide most of the basin

Vernal pool

Types of water bodies

![Bank side reservoir]

of the reservoir. Dams are usually located at a narrow section of a valley. The valley walls act as a natural container with the dam located at the narrowest point.

Bank-side reservoir: When the quantity of water in a river changes constantly, bank-side reservoirs are constructed to store the extra water pumped from the river. Such reservoirs are usually built partly by excavation and partly by the construction of a complete encircling bund or embankment. The London Water Supply System is one example of the use of bank-side storage for all the water that is taken from River Thames and River Lee.

Valley dammed reservoir

WATER

Service reservoir

Service reservoir: Service reservoirs store fully treated water close to a point of distribution. Many service reservoirs are constructed as water towers, often as elevated structures on concrete pillars where the landscape is relatively flat.

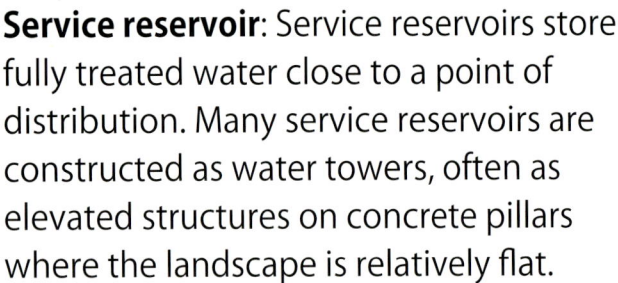
Five thousand years ago, the craters of extinct volcanoes in Arabia were used as reservoirs by farmers for their irrigation water.

Wetland

A **wetland** is an area of land whose soil is filled with water in form of moisture either permanently or seasonally. Such areas may also be covered partially or completely by

Wetland

shallow pools of water. The water found in wetlands can be saltwater, freshwater or a mixture. Pantanal in South America is the world's largest wetland covering an area between 140,000 sq km and 195,000 sq km. This tropical wetland lies mostly within the country of Brazil with portions extending to Bolivia and Paraguay.

Wetlands are characterized by a groundwater level that stands at or near the land surface long enough each year to support aquatic plants. Wetlands also provide a transition zone between dry land and water bodies. Different types of wetlands are: bog, marsh and swamps.

Bog

A **bog** is a type of wetland that gathers a deposit of dead plant material. Bogs occur where the water is acidic. Bog water has a brown colour.

A Quaking Bog

The main types of bogs are:

Valley bogs develop in gently sloping valleys or hollows. A stream may run through the surface of the bog.

Raised bogs develop from a lake or flat marshy area.

Blanket bog develops in cool climates with regular high rainfall. The ground surface may remain drenched almost all the time providing conditions for the development of a bog. In such conditions bog exists as a layer over much of the land, including hilltops and slopes.

Quaking bog occurs in wetter parts of valley bogs and raised bogs and sometimes around the edges of acidic lakes where a bog is beginning to form. Walking on the surface of a quaking bog causes it to move, thus the name 'quaking'. Bigger movements may even make the trees to sway.

Mire

> Mire is a low-lying wetland of deep, soft soil or mud with large algae covering the water's surface that sinks underfoot.

WATER

Swamp

Marsh

A **marsh** is a type of wetland that experiences frequent or continuous flooding. Usually, the water is shallow and grasses, rushes, reeds, sedges, other herbaceous plants and moss grows in this region. A marsh is different from a swamp, which has greater open water surface and is deeper than a marsh. The water of a marsh can be fresh, brackish or salty. Decomposition of plant materials in the water of the marsh often produces methane gas which self-ignites and is responsible for mysterious lights popularly known as **Will o' the wisps**, **Jack-o'-lanterns** or sprites. Methane is therefore also called marsh gas.

Swamp

A **swamp** is a type of wetland where large areas of land get covered with shallow bodies of water. A swamp generally has a large number of dry-land portions too. The two main types of swamp are **forest swamps** and **shrub swamps**. The water of a swamp may be fresh water, brackish water (a mix of freshwater and seawater) or seawater.

A common feature of swamps is water stagnation. Swamps are marked by very slow-moving waters. They are usually associated with adjacent rivers or lakes. In some cases, rivers become swamps for a distance.

Marsh

Types of water bodies

Flowing water bodies

Flowing water bodies are called so because they flow from one place to another.

Stream

A **stream** is a body of water with a current and a bed restricted within banks on both sides. A stream is named differently according to its certain characteristics or location.

Parts of a stream

Spring: The point in the ground at which a stream emerges from an underground source is called a spring. A stream can flow above the ground for some part of its course and underground for some part of its course.

In a spring, water flows to the surface of the Earth from underground. Thus, a spring is a site where the underwater

spring

surface meets the ground surface. A spring can be the result of surface water infiltrating into the Earth's surface and becoming a part of the groundwater.

 The study of streams and waterways is known as surface hydrology.

WATER

A source

Source: The source of a river or stream is the place from where the water in a river or a stream originates. The source is the farthest point of the river stream from its estuary, mouth or its junction with another river or stream.

Headwaters: The part of a stream or a river which is near to its source is called the headwaters.

Confluence: A confluence is a point in the course of two or more bodies of water where they meet together. It usually refers to the joining of tributaries. In case of two tributaries of approximately equal size, the confluence is called a fork.

Run: An almost smoothly flowing section of a stream is called a run.

Riffle: A riffle is a short, shallow part of a stream with a coarse bed over which the stream flows at a higher speed resulting in turbulence. Higher speed and turbulence results in small ripples. Riffles are usually caused by an increase in they stream bed's slope or an obstruction in the flow of the water.

Floodplain: That area of land near the stream which floods when a stream overflows its banks is called a floodplain.

Nickpoint: The point when the stream gradient experiences a sudden change.

Waterfall: The point where the stream falls

Confluence

Types of water bodies

over a sudden drop in the landscape is called a waterfall.

Mouth: The point at the end of stream's course at which the stream discharges its water into a large body of water such as a lake, sea or an ocean is called the **mouth**.

Mouth

Arroyo

Anabranch

An **anabranch** is a part of a river or stream that moves away from the main stream of the watercourse and rejoins the main stream downstream. Anabranches can result because of formation of small islands in the watercourse. Larger anabranches can last over a distance of several kilometres before rejoining the main channel.

> An arroyo is a dry river, creek or stream bed that temporarily or seasonally fills and flows after sufficient rain.

Bayou

Bayous are extremely slow-moving rivers or streams usually with an undefined shore. They are usually found in flat, low-lying regions. They are quite similar to a marsh. Bayous are commonly found in the southern United States, in the Mississippi River region.

Bayou

Canals

Canals are artificial channels for water. There are four types of canal:

25

WATER

Canal

Inter-basin canals are constructed to connect lakes, rivers, or oceans.

City canals form a part of a network of transportation in a city. Examples include the Canal Grande and other canals of Venice; the waterways of Bangkok etc.

Kettle

A **kettle** is a body of water formed by retreating glaciers or draining floodwaters which is shallow in depth and is full of sediment.

Aqueducts

Kettle

Aqueducts are water supply canals that are used for the transportation and delivery of water suitable for drinking for human consumption, municipal uses and agricultural irrigation.

Waterways are crossable transportation canals used for moving ships, boats and shipping goods and transporting people.

Kettles are formed as a result of blocks of ice breaking up from the front of a receding glacier and becoming buried by glacial outwash.

Stream pool

A **stream pool** is that part of a river or a stream where the water depth is more than the average depth of the stream and water velocity is below the average velocity. A stream pool may be that portion of the stream bed that is bedded with sediment or with gravels and in some cases the pool may have formed as basin. Plunge pools are stream pools formed by the action of waterfalls.

Stream pool

Rapid

Rapid

A **rapid** is that part of a river where the river bed has a steep incline causing an increase in water speed. A rapid is characterised by the river becoming shallower and having some rocks exposed above the flow surface. As flowing water splashes over and around the rocks, air bubbles mix with it and portions of the

White-water rafting

surface acquire a white colour, forming what is called 'whitewater' and hence the name whitewater rafting came into being.

Rapids occur where the bed material is highly resistant to erosion.

River

A **river** is a natural watercourse of freshwater flowing over the surface in channels towards an ocean, a lake, a sea or another river, usually fed along its course by converging tributaries. The existence of a river depends on three things— the availability of surface water, a channel in the ground and an inclined surface. In this sense the term 'river' includes all kinds of watercourses from the tiniest of brooks to the largest of rivers.

River

The shape, size and content of a river are constantly changing, forming a close relation between the river and the land it travels. On its way a river may carve through mountain ranges, create deep gorges and canyons, gentle valleys, lush meadows and mighty plains. Over time it may change drastically from a roaring, overflowing force in spring, to a still, icy-cold mass in the winter.

The water in a river is usually confined to a channel made up of a stream bed between banks. In larger rivers there is also a wider floodplain shaped by flood-waters. Flood plains can be very wide in relation to the size of the river channel. This distinction between river channel and floodplain can at times blur.

> The term upriver refers to the direction leading to the source of the river, which is against the direction of flow. On the other hand, the term downriver describes the direction towards the mouth of the river in which the current flows.

Youthful river is a river with a steep slope. It has very few tributaries and flows quickly. Its channels erode deeper rather than wider.

Youthful river

Mature river is a river with a slope that is less steep than those of youthful rivers and flows more slowly. A mature river is fed by many tributaries and has more discharge than a youthful river. Its channels erode wider rather than deeper.

Subterranean river

Mature river

Old river is a river with a low slope and low erosive energy. Old rivers are characterized by flood plains. (Examples: Huang He River, Ganges River, Tigris, Euphrates River, Indus River, Nile River)

Rejuvenated river is a river with a slope that is raised by movements inside the earth's crust.

Most rivers flow on the surface of the Earth however, **subterranean rivers** flow underground in caves.

An **ephemeral river** flows occasionally and can be dry for several years at a time. Some ephemeral rivers flow during the summer months but not in the winter.

Tidal creek

A **tidal creek** refers to that portion of a stream which discharges into an ocean, sea or a strait which is under the influence of ebb and flow of ocean tides. This part of the stream has changing levels of salt content in the water.

Creeks may often dry to a muddy channel with little or no flow at low tide, but often with significant depth of water at high tide.

Tidal creek

WATER

Waterway

A **waterway** is any navigable body of water including rivers, lakes, seas, oceans, and canals. A waterway must meet the following conditions:

1. The waterway must be deep enough to allow the draft depth of the vessels using it.
2. The waterway must be wide enough to allow passage for wide vessels.
3. The waterway must be free of barriers for navigation such as waterfalls and rapids.
4. The current of the waterway must be mild enough to allow vessels to make headway.

Vessels using waterways vary from small animal-drawn barges to huge ocean tankers and ocean liners, such as cruise ships.

Cruise ship

Distributary

A **distributary** is a stream that cuts off and flows away from a main stream course. They are a common feature of rivers. Distributaries usually occur as a stream near a lake or an ocean, but they can occur inland as well.

Tributary

A **tributary** is a stream or river which flows into a main river. A tributary does not flow directly into a sea, ocean or a lake. 'Right tributary' and 'left tributary' are terms stating the position of the tributary relative to the flow of the mainstream river. These terms are defined from the angle of looking at a river in the direction in which the water current is flowing.

Water way

Test Your MEMORY

1. What are the two types of water bodies?

2. What percentage of Earth is covered by oceans?

3. Name the five oceans of the world.

4. What is the name of the largest gulf in the world?

5. Name the longest bay of the world.

6. Which country is known as the 'Land of Thousand Lakes'?

7. What is a moraine?

8. Name the world's largest wetland?

9. Which gas is produced as a result of the decomposition of plant materials in water in a marsh?

10. What is a source?

11. What are canals?

12. Canal Grande in Venice and the water ways of Bangkok are examples of which type of canals?

Index

A
Antarctic Ocean 4
Atlantic Ocean 4

B
barrier island 10
Bay 4, 6, 7
bog 4, 20, 21

C
canals 3, 8, 25, 26, 30
cirque 17
coast 6, 7
coral reef 10
cove 4, 6

D
Distributary 30

E
entrance 6, 8
equator 5

F
fjord 4, 8, 10
floodplain 24, 28

H
harbours 3

I
Indian Ocean 4, 7
inlet 6, 8
Inter-basin 26

K
Kettle 26

L
lagoon 4, 8, 10

M
marshes 3
methane gas 22
Mill pond 13
Mire 21
moat 14
moisture 20

N
navigable 3, 8, 30

O
ocean 3, 4, 5, 7, 8, 9, 11, 25, 28, 29, 30

P
Pacific Ocean 4
plunge pool 4, 14
Pond 13, 16
ponds 3, 4, 11, 13, 16
puddles 3

R
rapid 27
reflecting pool 14
reservoir 13, 18, 19, 20
river 3, 8, 9, 11, 12, 18, 19, 22, 24, 25, 26, 27, 28, 29, 30

S
salinity 4
sand bar 10
sea 3, 4, 5, 6, 7, 8, 9, 10, 25, 28, 29
shore 5, 6, 7, 25
shoreline 7
sound 4, 8, 10
source 4, 23, 24
spring 18, 23, 28
Stream pool 14, 26
streams 3, 11, 23, 25
swamps 3, 20, 22
swimming pool 15

T
tarn 4, 17
tidal creek 29
tributaries 24, 28, 29

V
valley 8, 10, 18, 19, 21
Vernal pools 17, 18

W
water body 3, 8
waterways 23, 26, 30

* Maps not to scale; for illustration purpose only.